I w[ant to thank]
several people for their help
with this book.

First of all, thanks to
my husband Ed for the photos
and the moral support.

And thanks to my sister and
best friend, Joanne Moryl.
Without her expert help this
would have been a lost cause.

Also, for bits and pieces of this
and that, thanks to Georgia Kula
and Penny Hedler.

Judith A. Woods

THOSE CRAZY CATS

Judith A. Woods

Judith A. Woods

Avian Publications
6380 Monroe St. NE
Minneapolis MN 55432

Bruce Burchett Publisher/Owner
www.avianpublications.com
bruce@avianpublications.com
Phone & fax 763-571-8902

National Library of Canada Cataloguing in Publication

Woods, Judith A.
Those Crazy Caiques / Judith A. Woods.

ISBN 0-910335-05-2

Production and Design

Silvio Mattacchione and Co. / Peter A. Graziano Limited
1251 Scugog Line 8, RR#1.
Port Perry, ON, Canada L9L 1B2
Telephone: 905.985.3555
Fax: 905.985.4005

silvio@silvio-co.com
graziano@lincsat.com
www.silvio-co.com

Chapter goes here

Introduction
Living wih Parrots:
A little sanity goes a long way

Parrots are enjoying increasing popularity in our society, as they are third most popular pet behind dogs and cats. But not all parrots make good pets, and not all humans make good parrot owners. Unlike dogs and cats, parrots have not been domesticated for thousands of years, and general knowledge of their needs, while growing every day, is still scanty.

Unfortunately, the growing interest in acquiring a parrot has resulted in many of them being discarded due to unrealistic expectations of new owners. Parrots are not sweet, cuddly, obedient creatures that will respond to our every whim. They are still wild, and in their natural habitat, the prey of many species. Therefore, their first and most important instinct is flight for survival. Birds in captivity are constantly on the lookout for danger, as they are in the wild. So they are easily startled, quick to fly away (or attempt flight), and very quick to bite in defense.

Anyone who lives with birds must be aware of these facts and learn to understand the bird's body language. Also necessary is an understanding of their needs and actions in the wild and how these translate into captivity.

This is not an easy task. It takes time and effort: potential owners must read about parrots, and observe and interact with them. Never should a bird be purchased on impulse, no matter how cute and cuddly that baby in the pet shop may seem.

But approached with common sense, the correct expectations, and enough knowledge, living with a bird can be an absolute joy! Nothing provides more entertainment and amusement than the antics of a well-raised and cared for parrot. It doesn't matter what size or color, parrots can be great pets in the right hands.

Not all birds are right for everyone and choosing the best type of bird for you will depend on many factors: how much space you have for the bird and its cage; how much noise you can tolerate (and how close your neighbors are!); how much time you have each day to spend with the bird, and, not the least of all, your budget. The varieties available are almost unlimited, from the tiny parakeet in a 16-inch by 16-inch cage to the huge Hyacinth Macaw in a cage at least 4 feet by 3 feet.

Let's consider noise, which is subjective. Some people think Cockatiels are noisy. Cockatiels have a lovely musical sound, especially compared to a room full of screaming breeder Sun Conures. Any bird will make noise sometimes, but some are much more vocal than others, and some much louder than others. As a general rule, South American species such as Conures, Amazons, and Macaws are considerably noisier than African birds such as Greys, Senegals, Jardines, Meyers, and Lovebirds. The Australian and Indonesian species (Cockatiels and Cockatoos) are somewhere in between.

An extremely important consideration when buying or adopting a pet bird is the amount of time you have to devote to its psychological needs. All tame birds need daily interaction with their owners, but some require more than others. Those in the Cockatoo family, for example, have a reputation for pulling out their own feathers when ignored. Once the feather-picking habit is established, it is difficult, if not impossible, to break.

Birds such as Conures, Caiques, Amazons, Parakeets, and Cockatiels are better pets for folks with less time to spare. These species will be fine all day in their cages with lots of toys, provided they are given plenty of attention and human interaction out of their cages in the evening. In this case, it would be much better to house two birds of the same species together so they have each other for company during the owner's absence.

Finally, budget is an important consideration when choosing a pet bird. Parakeets can be purchased for relatively little money, as can the cages and supplies to house and care for them. The large Macaws can cost thousands of dollars, as can their cages. All birds should be checked annually, at the very least, by an avian vet, so vet fees must be considered too.

The best way to purchase a pet bird is to visit bird shops and breeders often. See the birds in your price range, ask numerous questions, play with the babies, learn about bird care, observe the cleanliness of the shop or breeding facility, and inquire about how knowledgeable the staff is and the diet fed to the youngsters. Read everything you can about birds, and talk to other bird owners.

Once you have decided on the type of parrot you would be comfortable living with, and have determined the amount of time and money you have available to devote to this kind of pet, visit as many sources as you can find. Concentrate on your chosen species, and read, study, and ask questions and more questions. You can never know too much about parrots. Everything you learn before you purchase or adopt will be extremely valuable during your years of living with a bird.

I decided to write this book because in all the years I have raised and lived with parrots, the only available information on Caiques has been a few articles in bird magazines and anecdotes from breeders and the few owners out there. Anyone who decides to live with a Caique should have a thorough understanding of what he or she is in for, both trouble and joy. I hope this book will serve that purpose.

CHAPTER 1
About Caiques: Where do these cheeky little imps come from?

My favorite species of parrot is the South American Caique (pronounced ky-eek). It is a small bird with a very big personality. There are two species. The first is the Black-Headed Caique, of which there are two subspecies: Pionites Melanocephala, with orange thighs; and Pionites Melanocephala Pallida, with yellow thighs, both of which generally inhabit the north side of the Amazon River in Peru, Colombia, Venezuela, and Guiana. The second is the White-Bellied Caique, which has three subspecies: Pionites Leucogaster, with green thighs; Pionites Leucogaster Xanthomeria, with yellow thighs; and Pionites Leucogaster Xanthries, with yellow thighs and tail feathers. These inhabit the south side of the Amazon River in Brazil, Bolivia, and southeastern Peru.

Caiques are small (9.5 in.), stocky birds weighing 145-165 grams. Their colors are beautiful, and all subspecies have white bellies and green wings. Black-Headed Caiques have orange or yellow thighs, yellow and orange under the wings, orange and yellow on the nape and throat, and black caps on their heads. The White-Bellied Caiques are similar except for their beautiful apricot-colored heads and the variation in thigh color. Both these species are truly outstanding-looking little birds with a life span of approximately 30 years.

The personality of these birds has been described as many things: clownish, impish, stubborn, opinionated, tenacious, affectionate, intelli-

Satchmo, P.L. Xanthomeria (left) showing yellow thighs. Phoebe. P. Melanocephala (right) showing orange thighs.

Hanging upside down.

gent, rowdy, bratty, crafty, conniving, captivating, arrogant, confident, and crazy, among others, and every one of these descriptions is true. They truly seem to have no "off" switch and can play for hours. Their play is unique among parrots in that they toss, tumble, hop, hang, climb, and run, all at breakneck speed.

Caiques walk upright like little penguins, and actually strut rather than walk. They are extremely willful little characters. Their philosophy of life is that no one EVER tells them what to do, and no one EVER stops them from doing what they want to do. Owners of these birds must be aware of their character traits and remain in control with firmness and kindness at all times. Caiques must be taught the "up" and "down" commands, and boundaries must be instituted for them or they will end up ruling the household.

These small birds are not considered to be very noisy, but in this writer's experience, they can be compared to Conures. Noise is relative for everyone, and some folks may not mind the vocalizations of Caiques. They have minimal talking ability, but are experts at imitating household noises and whistling tunes. Everything from the microwave oven, to the alarm clock, to the telephone will be mimicked very quickly, and some tunes are very easy for them to pick up. Also, laughing in imitation of the owner is common, and very comical. My Caiques imitate my Sun Conures with an awful racket, and I'd actually rather hear the Suns yell than that imitation, which is done with a raspy, throaty element that is really trying to the eardrums. Caiques may speak a few words, but usually in a high-pitched squeaky voice that is hard to understand. My oldest one, Gracie, learned to say "Go potty, Augie" when I was training a puppy, and then she'd say "Good boy, Augie!!" But she said it many times over before I realized what she was saying.

I cannot emphasize enough the incredible playfulness of these small parrots. They are truly the clowns of the parrot world. But in spite of this, and their reputation for fearlessness, they are no different from any other parrot in their approach to life and humans. They still have the prey instinct, which causes them to be immediately wary of anything in their environment that is unfamiliar. Consequently, these little birds will inflict a nasty bite if startled or frightened. Of course, they all vary in personality. I have one pair of Caiques in which the hen is extremely careful about approaching anything new I put in her cage. But her mate is much more adventuresome, and will almost immediately inspect anything new, which seems to give the hen the green light to go ahead and check it out. It's really interesting to watch. The entire time she is waiting for him to give the ok, she is whistling constantly, every tune she knows, which for her is a sign of extreme nervousness. This is just one bird's way of reacting to new things. Others will simply hide as far away from the object as possible, and some will attack instantly, putting the hands of the installer at risk.

Some Caiques are very nervous around people they don't know.

Again, my hen will start whistling all her tunes when she sees a stranger. This is a result of less and less exposure to new people as she has grown older.

The baby Caiques I hand-raised in my bird shop were just the opposite with strangers. They would all clamor for everyone who approached to pick them up and cuddle them. They were so used to people that they wanted to be with them all the time. The best situation for young Caiques who are well socialized is to continue their exposure to lots of different people after they are in their new homes. Let all your friends and visitors gently approach your Caiques and ask them to step up. Your birds will stay well socialized with this behavior, and will be less apt to bite out of fear.

But keep in mind that biting out of fear is not the only reason Caiques bite. These willful little imps insist on having their own way and will nip to get it. Remember, the bird's point of view is that you NEVER stop a Caique from doing whatever it wants, so gentle, firm control is extremely important. You can achieve this control by being consistent in your training of the birds. They must learn the "up" and "down" commands. They must also learn what is and is not acceptable behavior. Caiques like to use their beaks on fingers and body parts (as well as everything else–these are very "beaky" birds), so it's best to have toys or some kind of chewable available to distract them. They often bite and beak too hard from excess energy, so this is not a punishable offense. Diversion is the best tactic. But sometimes this behavior is caused by what I call "Caique overload" or just too much excitement for the bird to handle, and it results in nervous biting, which can be handled by a brief, quiet time-out to calm down.

CHAPTER 2
Places to Purchase:
You can't be too careful

Once the decision has been made to live with a Caique, after careful consideration of the time, effort, and financial obligations required, the best place to look for a bird is a breeding facility or a reputable bird shop.

With breeding facilities, the best recommendation is word of mouth. Talk to other customers of the facility and gauge their satisfaction with the health of the bird, the friendliness of the bird, the willingness of the owner to teach prospective buyers about Caique care, and the follow-up information and help you will receive after the sale. If possible, you should visit the facility often to watch your chosen baby grow to weaning. Under no circumstances should you buy an unweaned baby unless you are an experienced hand-feeder. Baby Caiques have an extremely powerful

Feeding a baby Caique.

feeding response and can be easily aspirated,* which, in most cases, causes death. Hand-feeding cannot be learned in a few minutes. It takes lots of practice, preferably with easier babies to feed than Caiques.

Keep in mind that many times a breeding facility will keep a "closed" aviary in order to prevent disease in its flock. This policy has to be respected and you must not expect to see an entire facility, especially the area where breeding birds are housed. Visitors can upset breeding birds enough to cause them to kill or abandon their young. But you do need to see babies in order to buy one. My belief is that you should not buy a parrot of any age that you cannot handle and spend time with. So follow the breeder's policies, and make sure you wash your hands thoroughly before entering a breeder's premises. I also recommend that you not visit more than one facility in a short span of time. Visit one, then go home and wash and change clothes before visiting another, in order to minimize the chance of transferring germs from one aviary to another.

If you patronize a bird shop—and there are good ones out there—the same principles apply. Visit often and take note of the cleanliness of the shop. Discuss their philosophy about bird ownership with the staff. Try to observe a feeding time to determine if the birds are handled and cuddled while being fed, instead of just having a syringe shoved down their throats before moving on to the next baby. These early weeks are crucial in the formation of the personality of the adult bird. Also crucial is how the babies are handled during the feeding process: with love and gentleness, or roughly, with no regard for individual needs.

Find out what the after-sale policy is at the shop. The staff must be willing to answer any and all questions that may arise long after you take your baby home. And the best shops will have a return policy of some kind, just in case circumstances change or the bird does not work out in your home. This policy will prevent a bird from being passed on to just anyone, especially someone who may not have the knowledge or interest in caring for it properly.

Another great way to find a source for your parrot baby is word of mouth. Ask your bird-owning friends where they purchased their birds, and find out what they think of the seller. Are they happy with the bird? Was it fully weaned before they were allowed to take it home? Were they fully instructed in its care? Were they taught everything they needed to know about feeding?

In the case of Caiques, did the seller emphasize the need for a large cage? Did they learn about toys— what kind and how many, and how often to rotate? All these questions are

* To cause formula to go into the trachea and into the lungs instead of the esophagus and the stomach, causing pneumonia and death.

White Belly babies approx. 6-7 weeks old.

critical to the health and happiness of the bird when it reaches your home. And perhaps the most important question is whether the seller is available AT ALL TIMES after the sale for questions and help. There will definitely be many questions as you learn to live with and care for your baby, even if you think you've asked everything you can to start with. There will also be moments of sheer panic, when you will frantically call your seller for advice and help, probably when your baby pulls some hair-raising stunt, or plays upside down on the floor of the cage with feet straight up making you think he/she is dead. Caiques love to play that way, and the first few times you see it can cause instant insanity.

Even if you are a more experienced bird owner and don't panic easily, your seller should be available for questions and help when you need it.

I should add a word here about purchasing or adopting an older bird. Sometimes it happens that circumstances change and a person can no longer keep a pet. In these cases, it is difficult to find a good home for the bird, as most people want a baby that they can raise themselves. But older birds can make wonderful additions to your family, if chosen carefully. The first requirement is to make sure the bird is healthy. Ask the former owner for the name of the vet who has cared for the bird. Every bird should have an annual checkup by a qualified avian vet. Contact the vet and ask for his/her opinion about the bird's health.

Second, talk to the owner about the bird. Find out why the bird must be sold or placed. Is it a biter? Is it noisy? Is the bird attached to only one family member and biting the others? None of these situations is a reason not to adopt or purchase, but it's best if you know exactly what you are getting into. Any of these problems can be fixed with love and patience and the right training. On the other hand, if a bird is feather-plucking to the point of drawing blood, only an experienced bird person should take it on. Lots of work and special care and know-how are required to help a bird like this to recover. Any bird that is being kept in neglectful or abusive circumstances is one that should be purchased or adopted by knowledgeable people. But many others are being re-homed from clean, nurturing homes and these birds make wonderful pets. They may take a little time to adjust to the change, but they will surely bond with their new owners if given the time. It is a myth that parrots only bond to whomever hand-feeds them, or to their first owner after weaning. Parrots readily re-bond with humans at any time in their lives.

CHAPTER 3
Coming Home:
Strange places are scary

Okay, you've decided on a Caique, and you've found a clean, reputable breeder from whom to purchase. And, best of all, this breeder has a clutch of Caique babies just five weeks old. So, now what?

The next step is to select one or two (recommended) of the babies. How, you ask? Play with them all, one at a time. You'll soon pick out one or two that just seem to "click" with you. Lots of bird owners swear that their birds chose them, instead of the other way around. But either way, you'll know. The babies that scamper quickly to you every time you approach; those that cuddle under your chin when you hold them; the ones that climb up to your head and rub their whole bodies through your hair; the ones that become "glue-footed" on your finger when you try to put them down, are the birds on which to concentrate. And these same youngsters will affectionately rub their faces all over your hands when you pick them up.

Once you've made a decision, visit your new baby (ies) as often as possible. Play with them at each visit. Try to plan visits during their feeding times. It's lots of fun to watch baby birds being hand-fed. Depending on the feeding method, it can be a really messy event, but it's still great to see. Syringe feeding isn't too messy, but spoon feeding can be a "formula fiasco." However, some breeders prefer this method. It enables them to handle each chick for a longer period of time, since it's a time-consuming process. It is also less likely to result in aspiration of the chick than syringe feeding.

White Belly baby with full crop.

But the most important factor that you should look for is not so much the method of hand-feeding, but the breeder's interaction with the babies. Good breeders feed slowly. They talk to the youngsters, stroke them a lot, clean their little faces gently, and are able to judge the correct amount of formula to give—not too much and not too little. Never buy a baby parrot that has been tube-fed. This method of feeding involves inserting a tube all the way into the crop: it results in little or no interaction or nurturing of the infant, and can cause crop and esophagus damage.

Another important consideration is the breeder's policy on weaning. Hopefully, he or she will never sell an unweaned baby except to an experienced hand feeder. If the breeder is selling babies before full weaning, find another source from which to purchase.

Hopefully, your breeder will require you to wait for full weaning, and patience on your part is in order. Baby Caiques are slow weaners and can take up to sixteen weeks to be fully weaned and eating enough on their own.

Caique babies often regress in the hand-feeding process. They will be fully weaned and eating on their own until you take them home, which to them is a strange place. Their reaction to the strangeness will often be to stop eating on their own and fall back to crying for hand-fed formula. Your seller should be ready to offer advice if this happens. There are several ways to handle the situation. You can offer formula on a spoon. You can feed human baby food warmed up, also on a spoon. Sometimes just the warmth and softness of that will satisfy youngsters' cries. But more often than not, holding and cuddling is all the babies need to be reassured that all is well in the new place. Never try to hand-feed a baby bird if you're not experienced. If these measures don't work, your seller must be willing to take the youngsters back to hand-feed for another week or so, until they are a little more mature and a little less needy.

Have the cage all set up with toys and dishes before you bring your new baby (ies) home. Perches should be close to the floor of the cage to provide a sense of security and eliminate fear of falling, although the birds may surprise you and be climbing all over the cage on the first day. In that case, arrange your perches at varying heights with one close to the food and water dishes. Toys should be hung at different angles and heights in the cage and should not be too heavy, so when a bird swings a toy it does not get knocked in the head on the rebound. Later, toys can be bigger and heavier as your babies learn to slam toys and get out of the way.

Black-Headed siblings on their playpen.

For the first few hours, leave the bird(s) in the cage to acclimate to it and the surroundings. You should approach the cage slowly and speak to them quietly and reassuringly. Some babies will sit rather paralyzed on the perch at first because a change of environment is quite traumatic for them. They go from familiar people and surroundings with their clutch mates to total strangeness, including people and cage, without their siblings. But Caiques being the nosy little moppets they are, will soon be exploring the cage and its contents with excitement. Let them. Let them proceed at their own pace, and they will settle in nicely.

During the first few days of living with these critters, try to follow the same routine. Uncover the cage at the same time each morning. Feed at the same time each day. Play with the birds around the same time each day. This will give them a sense of security because they will learn what to expect and when to expect it. I must caution you about overhandling any bird in the first few days you have it home. Many new owners make the mistake of spending numerous hours playing and interacting with a new pet at first. Then reality sets in and we all have to go to work and/or do things away from the bird or out of the house. You really don't want your birds to come to expect constant attention because you will have troubled birds on your hands when you can no longer give that much.

During the first few days at home, approach each of your babies with your index finger extended under the bird's chest and say "up-up" or "step-up." This is the most important lesson the birds will ever learn.

Caiques amusing themselves.

Hopefully, your breeder has already taught this command, but you need to keep reinforcing it. It should be an automatic response from a bird to raise its foot up when you say the words and/or extend your finger. This is the famous "up-up command" taught by the well-known behaviorist Sally Blanchard, and is part of her training technique called "nurturing dominance." It consists of gentle training using treats as rewards at first with no punishment at all for mistakes. This method gives you, the bird parent, the control that is absolutely necessary, especially with willful Caiques, and produces happy, well-adjusted birds.

Another word on routines. It's important to establish routines when you bring a bird home for the first time, as it provides the feeling of security it needs. But too rigid a system is not good for birds either. As your birds settle into their new home, and you are sure they are feeling comfortable and eating well, start to vary the schedule somewhat. This will prevent your birds from freaking out when there is an unexpected change that is out of your control. I made this mistake with my first bird—a little Sun Conure girl named "Ernie." When she was little, I rarely took her out of the room that housed her cage. Consequently, when I did, she was petrified.

Some practices should never vary. Feeding should be at approximately the same time each day, as should bedtime. But playtime can be at many different times during the day. Your birds should also learn to be content at times to stay in their cage while you are doing things in the same room. As much as Caiques need attention, they should not become used to getting it constantly.

You will find your own schedule as you settle in with the birds. Whatever works well for you is what your birds must adapt to, and most do so with little trouble.

Remember, Caiques need lots of toys and mental stimulation, and preferably a cage-mate. Leave a radio or TV on when you must be out for any length of time. Your birds will develop their own routine for when you are not there–eating, bathing, playing, napping. So relax and enjoy their antics. YOU will probably never watch TV again!

CHAPTER 4
Feeding:
Keeping these little "Hoovers" healthy

"Feeding" sounds like an easy chapter to write about. The fact is that feeding a parrot is a difficult task in light of all the information and misinformation that is out there. You will find all kinds of conflicting theories on the subject in everything you read.

Twenty years ago, everyone thought a parrot's diet consisted of seed and water, even in the wild. At that time, parrots did not have a long life expectancy in captivity. When researchers realized that parrots in the wild lived much longer than those in captivity, they began to look at the diets of wild parrots. Of course, most parrots back then were wild caught, and the shock of capture and transport to the pet trade killed a large number of them. But even the ones who survived to live in people's homes didn't live as long as they should.

Researchers began to follow birds in the wild and observe their eating habits. They found that parrots eat a large variety of foods throughout the year, traveling from place to place and foraging according to the season and what is available at a given time at a certain place. But since this is a difficult, if not impossible, situation to

duplicate, they were at a loss, and seed remained the mainstay of captive parrots' diets.

About twelve years ago, pellets were invented. Pellets are little nuggets that contain lots of minerals, vitamins, and other nutrients. They are a grain-based food manufactured into little pieces, and have a lot of the nutrition known to be needed by parrots. For a long time after their introduction to the parrot food industry, they were considered to be the complete food for birds, and most of the companies that made them promoted them as the only diet needed for your bird. And it was certainly evident that birds who ate pellets seemed to be healthier and longer-lived than those on seed alone. But as the research into wild parrots continued, it was obvious that this was not the whole story. Parrots on pellets were living longer, healthier lives, but still not as long as in the wild. So research continued, and it continues today. The current consensus on parrot feeding is that the most important factor in a captive bird's diet is a variety of live foods. By live foods I mean fresh greens, grains, fruits, vegetables, sprouts, some flowers, some stems of flowers. Birds in the wild move from place to place with the seasons, and eat different foods at different times according to what grows in the area they are inhabiting. Seeds are also an important part of the diet, and some parrots occasionally eat insects as a source of protein.

The problem with feeding these creatures in captivity is that no matter what you put in front of a bird to eat, it will pick out its favorite foods and leave the rest. If you feed seed with other foods, the first item consumed is the seed because they like it the best and then they are too full to bother with fruits, vegetables, or pellets. These items then become toys to toss around the cage and sometimes even the room. The next day the owner comes in and empties the dishes and provides fresh everything, including seed. The bird again eats the seed and plays with the rest.

Many books on feeding parrots tell you to feed fifty percent pellets, forty percent table food, and ten percent seed. Or eighty percent pellets, twenty percent table food, and no seed. Or sixty percent pellets, twenty percent table food, and twenty percent seed. No matter which of these formulas you use, the question still remains: How do you know what percent of each item your bird is eating? And how much is he/she really ingesting after some falls on the floor and some gets flung around the cage? I have pondered the question for years, never knowing for sure what the correct answer is for my birds.

When I first started keeping birds I fed seed and water, not knowing any better. Years ago, that was staple diet for all birds. As time went on and I learned more, I tried to convert my birds to pellets. Most were extremely resistant to this idea! They seemed to just stare at the pellets wondering what they were, having no idea they were food. So I tried mixing seed and pellets together. Day after day I threw out bowls full of pellets and seed hulls, which told me they were fishing out all the seeds and ignoring the pellets. I tried several kinds of pellets thinking they may just accidentally ingest one and find they liked it. I tried the pellets with bright colors produced by food coloring, the plain uncolored pellets, pellets in all shapes and sizes. While my birds would all taste the ones with color, they never really ate many of them. They would stubbornly wait for me to supply some seed. I have one Sun Conure who will not eat anything at all if I don't provide some seed. She will eat her fruits and veggies as long as the seeds are coming, but she will not touch a pellet.

Caiques, however, have a reputation for being excellent eaters. They are affectionately known among Caique breeders and owners as "Little Hoovers" or "Little Garbage Cans" or "Little Vacuum Cleaners," because once they know an item presented is food they will eat it. Caiques will eat

A few of the healthy foods for your bird.

Once again, you can only make an educated guess on this, so the best advice I can give is to feed your Caiques lots and lots of healthy table food in the morning, along with a bowl of fresh, clean water. One of the key factors in feeding table food is to feed as big a variety as you can get your hands on, and preferably organic only. I know this is difficult, but do your best. If you can't find everything organic, try organic baby food without additives. Otherwise, make sure you wash thoroughly everything you offer your birds. There is a list of healthy live foods in Appendix 1. Since some

ANYTHING, including things that are not food and anything that is not nailed down. This is a wonderful plus for the Caique parent, as these birds are relatively easy to feed.

But we still have the percentage question to deal with. Caiques love to dunk their food in their water dishes. I think they think they are related to raccoons. But in dunking everything they make a tremendous mess all over the cage, so it's difficult to tell how much is going into the bird.

One of the many pellet varieties.

Some of the dry foods for your bird.

food dishes. Then in the afternoon, the seed and other dried foods is a treat.

This is the closest I can come to duplicating what birds eat in the wild. I try to vary the things I buy for their fresh food dish each week to keep their interest up. Some birds do not like changes in their diets (or anything else, for that matter), but Caiques relish a variety of foods. Once they recognize an item as food, they will gladly eat it. Sometimes a new food will throw them for a loop, but if they see you eating it they will understand that it's food and follow suit. And birds take their cues from people, so show some excitement when eating that piece of broccoli or leaf of kale!

Caiques have a few special needs besides the regular needs of all parrots. They are a particularly energetic species of bird, always on the go, playing, swinging, running, hopping. Because of this increased energy output, they have a slightly greater need of fruit in their diets, much like Lories, who require lots of fruit and nectar. Caiques also love nectar and it's good for them, as is fruit juice. Try

foods are more nutritious than others, it is a good idea to put in a bowl of just the most nutritious foods once or twice a week, to make sure they are getting as much as possible of the good stuff.

Leave the fresh food in your bird's cage for several hours (less if it's hot in the room). Then remove it, and put in a dish of dried foods consisting of some pellets, some seeds, some dried fruits, etc. The Appendix also contains a list of these dried foods.

At this time, clean and refill your bird's water dish, as you will find it disgustingly dirty from the morning dunking. And, of course, the little monkeys will begin dunking all over again with their dry food! I find this system works well for me because my birds are really hungry in the morning and will gladly eat from their fresh to include some in their diets once or twice a week.

We need to refer back here for a moment to discussion of the breeder or shop from which you purchase your babies. A properly raised and weaned baby Caique will come to your home already eating a tremendous variety of foods that he/she loves. It is the sign of a reputable and caring breeder or shop that they have raised the baby with an abundance of healthy foods. How a baby parrot learns to eat on its own will have a profound and lasting effect on its eating habits for the rest of its life.

Research into parrot nutrition has also shown that birds spend much of their day in the wild foraging for food. Obviously, it is not set out before them in a convenient bowl. Parrots also need the physical stimulation of a varied diet including many different shapes, textures, and natural colors. Since foraging occupies such a large part of their time, it is wise to set up foraging situations in your bird's cage. This can be done in many ways. There are numerous toys on the market that allow you to hide bits of food so your bird has to work to get them. You can also clip pieces of food to the wire of the cage in various places, using different items such as kale or spinach leaves, or hunks of fruit like melon or orange. Try wrapping foods around toys. Use kabobs for piercing food and hanging in the cage. And try putting soaking wet leaves of various

greens on the top of the cage. Caiques love this and will have great fun eating and making a mess. (Well, I never said Caiques weren't messy birds! As a matter of fact, "messy" is at the top of the list of their characteristics!)

If you are converting a bird, baby or older, to a more healthy diet, take your time. Do not rush the process. Cold turkey is extremely hard on a bird, especially one who is already under tremendous stress from moving from one home to another. Share your healthy meals at the table (or on a play stand near the table for finicky folk), let your bird watch you eat foods the bird has never seen before. Birds are social eaters. They eat in groups. So eat with your bird. And gradually replace less healthy foods with more healthy ones.

Just a word of caution before moving on. I'm sure you are all aware of the foods that are absolute no-nos for any bird. But a reminder never hurts, especially since I am encouraging you to feed such a variety of fresh food to your bird. No bird should EVER have avocado, chocolate, or alcohol. Other items that are not good are heavily salted or sugared foods, dairy products in excess, greasy foods, etc. In other words, if it's not so good for you, don't feed it to your bird. Common sense applies here. An occasional French fry is not going to kill you or your bird, but a steady diet of them is bad for both of you.

A word about droppings is appropriate here. The color and consistency of bird's droppings is largely dependent on what the bird consumes. So don't be alarmed if the droppings seem wetter when your bird eats more fresh food. This is not diarrhea, but just increased urine from more water in the food. As long as there are still solids and white urates in the droppings, your bird is fine. And color, too, plays a large part. A bird eating papaya will have very orange droppings. Perfectly normal!

Again, Caiques are good eaters. They will try pretty much anything you give them. They love fresh fruits and will express their gratitude by making pleasing jungle sounds while digging in. So have fun, give them a great variety of healthy foods, and dig in with them. You'll both be healthier for it.

CHAPTER 5
Housing:
There's no place like a BIG home

Keep in mind that the cage you buy now could be your bird's home for many years to come. You might as well start out right, since changing cages is somewhat traumatic for birds, just like moving to a new home is difficult for you. The cage should be the biggest you can afford and have room for in your home. There is no such thing as a cage too big for a bird. Caiques are high-energy birds that are on the move constantly, and need lots of room to climb and play. The only thing that might be too big is the bar spacing. For Caiques and similar-size birds the bar spacing should be no more than three-quarters of an inch. Half-inch spacing will also work. Anything wider than three-quarter-inch will enable your bird to stick its head through the bars, and this can be very dangerous, if not fatal, if the head gets caught.

There are many types of cages available today and the list is growing all the time. Visit pet shops, the Internet, and bird specialty shops, and ask for advice on the cages they carry. Some cages are easier to service and clean than others. Some cages have dish openings in the front, some on the side. Depending on where you position the cage, this dish placement could be an important factor. If you place a cage in an alcove or close to another piece of furniture, then side access dishes are difficult to use.

Most cages today are square or rectangular, and some have fancy tops or playpen tops where a bird can spend time outside of its cage. The choice you make should fit in with your life style and space. Round cages are not used much anymore because the bars converge at the top on many models and this can be dangerous, even for small birds, if heads get caught. So stay away from them. There are too many other types of cages out there.

Cage material must be considered. Make sure that the cage you choose is made of nontoxic materials, with no danger of lead or zinc poisoning from chewed or chipping paint. Cages should be longer than they are high, as this provides more play area for the birds.

Placement of the cage in your house deserves a lot of consideration. The bird should not be isolated from the family and the activity in the house, but he/she should also not be in the way, or in the middle of lots of action and turmoil, which can cause stress. A happy medium is desirable. Your bird needs to be a part of the family and see and hear all that's happening, but not be placed where people will be tripping over the cage or racing past at high speed.

Another bad place to put the cage is near a door, which can cause more stress and which subjects the bird to drafts each time the door is opened. Some birds will enjoy being placed by a window so they can see out, and some will be stressed or frightened by this. Use your judgment and read your bird's body language to determine if this is true. A stressed or agitated bird will be edgy and bitey and have difficulty sitting still. It will also not eat properly.

The inside of the cage deserves as much consideration as its placement in the room. Toys are an integral part of a Caique's life and must be placed with care. The toys themselves will be discussed in the next chapter, but the placement of toys is what we're considering here.

The first rule of toy placement is not to put them directly over food dishes. Caiques like to hang and swing like little acrobats, and will poop in the food dishes

repeatedly if they are under the toys. The same rule applies to perches—never over the food dishes. Toys should be spaced out around the cage with many in close proximity to the perches for easy access.

Perches should be of varying diameter. This provides flexibility for the bird's feet. A concrete perch is useful for keeping the bird's nails from becoming too sharp. However, it's easy to forget the nails if they don't develop sharp points. They still need trimming when they grow, even if they don't prick your arm when you hold the bird. Concrete perches also serve to keep the birds' beak in good condition if placed near the food dishes. Caiques are incessant beak-rubbing birds, and will use the abrasive perch for cleaning the beak, which helps to keep it in good condition.

Gracie.

The cage should have at least three bowls: water, dry food, and wet food. A fourth bowl for talon toys is also a good idea. If you can teach your bird to drink from a bird bottle, it will always have a source of clean water. Make sure your bird knows how to drink from a bottle before you remove its water dish. My advice, however, is to provide both. Caiques think they are miniature raccoons and love to dunk everything they eat or play with, and it seems cruel to take away their water dish. But you must be willing to clean and refill that dish several times a day if you leave it in. So it's up to you. I tried using a water bottle with my female Caique Gracie. She spent two whole weeks reaching

Deeny on her playpen.

around to the outside of the cage trying to undo the bolt that held the bottle in place, never once drinking from it. I finally gave up and removed it.

When talking about cages, we need to discuss grates. Most cages come with grates to prevent birds from reaching dropped food and droppings. When the birds are very young, grates can be dangerous. Feet can get caught, and young birds fall easily from their perches and can get feet and wings caught in grates. When your bird is young, its perches should be low and the bottom of the cage padded. Use thick towels with paper towel over them to provide a soft surface to fall on.

When your bird matures, a grate is a matter of opinion and cage construction. Some cages must retain their grates or they provide a large escape area for the birds. In others, the use of the grate is optional. Personally, I don't need another item to scrub and disinfect in my bird cages, so I don't use grates. I find that Caiques are going to play on the bottom of the cage whether there is a grate or not and there is no way to keep them away from the debris down there. So I change the papers often to help keep things clean.

A word about playgyms is in order here. They are wonderful items to have, especially the kind that can be moved from place to place. This way your bird can be with you much of the time you are out of the room containing it's cage. But, a word of caution is important. When your bird is young, or when it's first introduced to the playgym, it has a tendency to repeatedly jump off. So you must supervise its time on the gym until you are sure the bird feels secure enough on it to stay. When your bird jumps off, pick it up with the "up-up" command and replace the bird on the gym. It will eventually get the idea that it needs to stay and will begin to explore the toys, food, and water you have put there for it.

The height of your playgym is a consideration too. Some birds become dominant in a position higher than your head. Some birds don't. My Caiques don't seem to register being higher than I am, which they are when on top of their cages, and I am six feet tall. But, I have known many other species of birds that have become pretty bossy up there. I've also read about Caiques that become Grand PooBah when higher than their owners. So you must know your own bird. If it tends to become bossy and aggressive when higher than your head, do not allow it up there. This applies to having the bird on your shoulder too. All birds are different, so there is no hard-and-fast rule, like "never let your parrot on your shoulder". Know your own bird and act accordingly.

One last word on playgyms: They are never a substitute for a cage. Many people would come into my bird shop and say, "It's cruel to confine a bird to a cage. It should stay out on its playgym all day. How would you like to live in a cage?" The answer, of course, is that birds LOVE their cages. They provide security and safety, and act as a den, just as a crate does for a dog. The dangers for a parrot uncaged all the time are too numerous to mention here, but just a few would be electrical cords to chew, dogs and cats, open toilets to drown in, hot pots on the stove to get burned in. You get the picture.

CHAPTER 6
Toys:
Play is hard work

Toys, toys, and more toys is the rule for Caiques. These birds are the most active little devils, and with that activity goes acrobatics and destruction. They will swing, climb, roll, somersault, hop, run, and chew, chew, chew. So lots of toys are an important part of their environment.

Toys that can be shredded are probably first choice with Caiques. And there are many, many toys out there for shredding. You can buy a tremendous variety of wood toys, plain, and/or colored with nontoxic materials. Wood strung on rope and leather is the best choice. Rope and leather can also be colorful, but make sure they are colored with nontoxic materials.

My Caiques' very favorite shredding toy is a whole roll of toilet paper. It can be put on a perch, or a plastic holder made specifically for the purpose, or it can be hung in the cage with a piece of rope or leather. One of my pairs will destroy an entire roll in a matter of hours, but the other pair will play with it on and off for days. You must be prepared for the mass of soft, chewed-up paper in the bottom of the cage, but these birds have such fun with it that it's well worth the mess. It's a wonderful, inexpensive toy for hours of fun.

Another good shredding toy is the inner core of cardboard from

Partially shredded roll of toilet paper.

paper towel or toilet paper rolls. Shoved between the bars, the birds will play with these extensively. You can also roll up a sheet of newspaper and weave it in and out of the cage bars. The birds love to play with this, pulling it out from the bars and ripping it to shreds.

Tree branches are another good toy for shredding, as well as climbing; but make sure they are pesticide free and of the nontoxic variety. Caiques love to peel off the bark and fling it around their cages. Branches should be taken from the ground a good distance from roadways, to avoid contamination from passing vehicles, road salt, and sand. To best prepare these branches for the birds, heat them in the oven at 250 degrees for an hour. This will kill any bugs that may be under the bark.

Climbing toys are crucial for Caiques. Most of their playtime is spent climbing, swinging, hanging by one claw, and jumping from one hanging toy to another. Rope perches and toys, ladders, swings, platforms, and all types of hanging toys are great for these activities. And, we should not forget, Caiques spend most of their time playing.

A play stand away from the cage is also a very good idea for these active birds. It should have lots of toys attached for them to climb on and play with, as well as dishes for food and water while they are away from their cages. A play stand is a great way to keep your bird occupied while you are busy doing things, but still want it to be near you. Birds must always be supervised while out of their cages. And birds on play stands will tend to jump or fly off until they are used to

it. Keep putting your bird back every time it comes off and it will soon learn that the play stand is a fun place to be, as well as where you want it to stay.

Puzzle toys are a big hit with most birds. Toys that require the bird to put an object onto another object, or toys that fit various pieces inside one another are great parrot toys. Some of the best puzzle toys also serve as foraging toys. Birds in the wild forage on and off all day for food. It is best to duplicate some of that activity in the caged environment to keep them as busy as possible. I have a toy that consists of two plastic halves, which set one on top of the other and form a cavity when together. One of my hens goes instantly to the toy, lifts up the top half with her beak, holds it up with a claw and takes a treat out of the toy. She will continue to hold the top up with her claw as she eats the food. My other Caiques just dump the top off to the side and eat the food out of the bottom.

There is another toy that serves as both a puzzle and a foraging toy. It's a wooden or acrylic device that holds nuts. There is only one small opening where the nuts fit in or out, and the bird has to work at getting the nut in exactly the right position to remove it.

These are two of many toys that your bird will love. But there are many objects around the house that provide fun for your bird and are

Gracie and Mikey in their toy-filled cage.

Hanging toys are another favorite of Caiques. Not only are they good for chewing and shredding; they serve as swinging toys as well. Caiques' favorite activity is to hang on a hanging toy and make it rotate by flapping their wings, and when not swinging in a circle, ferociously chew the toy.

inexpensive: tissue boxes with any plastic removed; paper towel and toilet paper rolls, either pushed through the bars of the cage or strung on rope or leather and hung in the cage; and small plastic containers with plastic beads inside with secure lids.

You can buy inexpensive things in the store that you wouldn't think of as toys for birds, but that serve well in this capacity. At your local lumber and hardware store you can buy sections of PVC pipe that will amuse your Caiques for hours. They love to run through and hide in them, or wrestle with each other in them. You can also buy chunks of untreated wood and either string them on rope or leather or just put them in the cage as talon toys. Caiques are extremely innovative birds and will make a toy of almost anything they can get their beaks on.

There are many, many toys available for your Caiques. Swings, ladders, bells, flavored chew blocks, big wiffle balls stuffed with fun chew materials, plain wood toys, brightly colored wood, plastic, and acrylic toys, talon toys of all kinds; and there is no end to the toys you can concoct from your own imagination. However, there are several rules to keep in mind for the welfare of your pets. All materials must be nontoxic. That means the chain and clip that hold the toy in place. The best material you can use for those parts of a toy is stainless steel. Some chains and clips have lead and/or zinc in their composition. Not all birds will actually chew those parts of a toy, but why take the chance? Even if your bird never has, there can always be a first time. It is better to be safe than sorry. Stainless steel is toxin free and completely safe. There are toy companies who specialize in stainless steel toys for birds, so check them out.

The next rule is to keep all rope materials trimmed. Birds can unravel a rope toy to such an extent that the individual strands are thin like thread and easily wrap around a foot or toe, trapping the bird. This is so traumatic for the bird that it can thrash itself into serious injury or death trying to free itself. The thin strands can also wrap around the bird's neck with the same result. Often when this happens the bird suffocates before help arrives. Keep all ropes trimmed short and tie short, thin ends together to make it impossible to trap the bird in any way.

I have found that the same problem can arise with fabric toys, and therefore I've stopped using them altogether for Caiques. My birds are particularly destructive of these substances and the fabric shreds more easily than rope. These toys are fine for other birds that do not shred so much of what they come in contact with. I still offer them to Cockatiels and Conures.

Another word on toys: Wash them frequently. Caiques never stay in one place more than a few seconds, especially when playing. So their toys will become pooped on and dirty in short order. While you're washing toys, wash perches too. Wiping their beaks while eating is another messy habit of all birds, so perches get very dirty as well.

And the last word on toys: Rotate, rotate, rotate. If you change the toys and the placement of them inside the cage every few days, your birds will act like you gave them brand new toys. It's a great way to keep them busy and happy and using up all that tremendous energy.

CHAPTER 7
Behavior and Training:
Dealing with power surges

One of the first discussions in this chapter should be natural behaviors. Much of what Caiques do and learn to do in captivity is based on natural behaviors for the species

First is walking. Caiques are not great flyers. They are heavy-boned birds for their size, and while they fly well enough in the wild, their flight in our homes is clumsy at best. The preferred method of mobility is walking, but their walk is extremely comical because it's actually a swagger. Caiques tend to walk upright like penguins, so the body sways from side to side.

Another natural behavior is hopping. Caiques are famous for hopping from place to place, and because it's so normal for them, it's easy to teach them to hop on cue. One of the most amusing sights I've ever seen is a Caique hopping around in or out of its cage. And what's even more entertaining is to watch two birds hopping around together. They will hop all over, then one will turn upside down on its back while the other hops over and lands on the first bird's belly. Lots of screaming and objecting ensues, and the resulting racket sounds like a murder in progress. But this is Caique

amusement. They love these rough-and-tumble games with each other. If you have two birds that play this way, don't let the noise scare you. These little monkeys are just playing with each other. The first time I heard this ruckus, I panicked and removed one bird from the cage, but I soon learned that this is normal for Caiques and no one will get hurt. So I just let them thrash each other for fun and they soon get bored with that and move on to the next game.

A young Caique playing on his back.

In the wild, Caiques, as well as many other South American species of parrots, sleep in hollowed-out tree cavities. They feel protected from the elements and predators this way, and the cavity provides a good nesting site when breeding time comes. In captivity, protected sleeping quarters is still a priority, so many will find a place within their cages as a substitute. If

Playing "Hide and go Seek".

you provide a box for roosting and/or nesting, it will serve the purpose. If you don't, the bird will often burrow under whatever is on the bottom of its cage, usually paper. So don't be alarmed if you walk up to your bird's cage some morning and see no bird, but a lump under the papers. When you move the paper you will find your baby upside down on his back with his feet straight up in the air. Don't panic!! He is not dead!! He is just sleeping peacefully.

Power surges are a definite happening with Caiques. This can also be called overload. These birds can become so excited that they go a little crazy and their behavior gets out of control. This is when most biting occurs, as well as other aggressive behaviors. I had an incident with my own young hen named "Deeny". I was away for almost three weeks and had left my birds in the care of very competent employees. When I returned, Deeny was very excited and rather hyper. I was standing next to one of her caregivers when she lunged for that person. I mistakenly (or maybe not) reached over to intercept her before she reached the other woman, and she bit my ring finger down to the bone. It was the worst bite I've ever experienced in all my years of aviculture. And I could not blame Deeny. I am not sure what was going on in her little head at the moment, but obviously the bite was not intended for Mommy, but for the other woman. The bite was so bad I passed out on

Phoebe (right) yelling at Satchmo (left).

the floor, but actually it required no medical attention. There is no doubt in my mind that this was a case of overload—all the excitement of seeing Mommy again, and the people around who wanted to see Deeny greet me after my absence just added up to too much excitement for her to handle.

Another reason for overload in a Caique is simple fatigue. A tired bird can be grouchy and its reactions to people may suffer. There are certain times in the day when your bird rests. Naps are frequent, and if you approach your bird during a nap it may be startled or just annoyed. It is best to let the bird rest if you see it napping.

Birds are creatures of habit. Yours will get used to its bedtime if it's approximately the same time each night that you put it to bed. If you then disturb him/her, or fail to settle the bird down within a reasonably close time, it may become grouchy. This is no different than people when we are tired or awakened suddenly – we get grouchy and disagreeable with others.

The best way to handle overload is to back off and let your bird cool down. Time alone in the cage is the best remedy for these power surges. It's no different for the bird than for us when too much information comes at us all at once. We feel like our heads are about to explode, and

the birds feel the same way. Give them a little space and quiet time, and they will be fine again. This situation happens with lots of parrots, but Caiques are especially prone to it, as they are somewhat hyper to begin with. One of the best ways to control overload is to approach your bird as calmly as possible. The bird senses your demeanor and responds to it calmly because it senses no aggression or fear or over-excitement on your part.

Another situation these birds get into involves a game called "Macho, macho, man." Caiques love to play this because they are pushy little critters anyway, and this game involves proving to you, the owner, that the bird is BOSS. The game goes like this: You are holding the bird on your hand and it starts to run up to your shoulder. You don't want the bird on your shoulder because you sense a little mischief in the air, and a mischievous bird does NOT belong that close to your face. But when you put your hand up to stop the climb, you get bitten. How dare you stop a Caique from doing what it wants to do??? Don't you know that this bird is always king/queen of its entire domain?? And to make matters worse, you have not only stopped the bird from doing what it wants, but you have very effectively made this bird angry, and that is usually worth another bite or two. You get the picture. This game could also be called "Who's in Charge??" And the answer is, your bird should never be in charge. Caiques need a firm, loving hand to keep their behavior acceptable, sometimes more so than other South American species. The truth is that birds don't really want to be in charge; they just think they do. What they really want is guidance from the flock leader. And the flock leader is you. Your bird will be a much happier member of your household with guidance and leadership from you. It makes its needs and wants known to you in bird language and behaviors, which is the only way it knows how. And if you take the time to learn what its natural behaviors are trying to tell you, you will both be happy. Clear, consistent messages every day about what are acceptable and what are not acceptable behaviors make your bird happier, because there is no confusion.

The guidance you provide as flock leader must be totally without force or aggression. Parrots are like two- or three-year-old children, unable to make the right behavior choices for living in captivity, because of the conflict between natural behaviors and living with humans. And, like children, they cannot foresee the consequences of their behaviors.

The single most important command you can teach our Caique is the "up-up" command. Also important is the "down" command. It may take some patience and understanding to teach this, but it's very important that

you do. To teach the "up" command, put your index finger against the bird's chest and say "up, up." If the bird doesn't respond, push gently against the chest right above the legs and say the command again. If you push gently, the bird starts to lose its balance and will automatically reach up for your finger with its foot to balance itself. Praise the bird once it steps up. Then put your bird back down on the perch saying "down" and using the same balance technique, only in reverse. If the bird does not get off your hand, tilt your hand just slightly to make the bird feel off balance and it will reach for the perch. Again, praise your bird. Practice this over and over. You can reward the behavior with a tiny piece of your bird's favorite food. After some practice, no reward is necessary, but you should always praise your baby when he/she does as you ask.

It is vitally important that you have this power over your bird with the "up" command. This will get the bird out of its cage whenever you want or need to take it out, and will maintain your status as flock leader. I hear story after story from bird owners who say, "My bird refuses to come out of his cage." These birds have never been taught the "up" command. Many of them can easily be taken out of their cages when they realize that you mean what you say. If an owner puts his hand in the cage and the bird tries to bite, the owner pulls his hand away. The bird learns that it takes nothing but a gesture of biting to get its own way. Lots of these birds will meekly step up if the owner would just not pull his hand away. Reaching in with confidence will teach the bird that you are serious.

Birds have an innate drive to protect their territory from others of their kind as well as from predators. And the cage becomes their territory in our homes. If they are allowed to become overly possessive or protective about the cage, you have the beginnings of a parrot becoming its own flock leader and getting out of hand. It is much harder to re-train a bird who is possessive of its cage than it is to teach the "up" command when it's young.

CHAPTER 8
Health:
I'm only sick when you're not looking

You should find an avian veterinarian before you bring your baby home. Your bird should be seen by a vet within a day or two of leaving its breeder. Finding a vet in an emergency is a trying experience, and some vets will not see you if the animal in question is not their regular patient. Also, some of the emergency animal clinics do not really know how to treat birds, but are often the only option. So, establish a relationship with an avian vet before you get your bird and hopefully that vet will be there for you if the need arises.

First, if you have other animals, ask that vet if she/he treats birds. If so, you are in luck. And if the vet is a certified avian vet, so much the better. If not, ask if your vet has a connection to a certified avian vet, upon whom he/she can call if required. If none of this applies, you must begin your search for a vet for your new bird.

First, ask your friends and acquaintances for a referral to a vet who treats birds. Word of mouth is the best recommendation. Call and make an appointment to meet and talk to this vet. Find out what the vet's experience and training are with birds. Discuss with him/her the policies of the practice—does the vet cover his/her own practice during off-hours? Does he/she share the practice with other vets? If so, are the other vets proficient in treating birds, or do you have to wait for this vet to be there? Does this vet believe in inoculating birds, and if so, what vaccinations does he/she recommend? There are only a few vaccinations for birds at the present time, and they are controversial. Any questions you have should be answered before you make a decision to trust the life of your bird to a vet. You need to feel confident about the doctor and comfortable putting your trust in the entire organization. Also inquire about fees, so you are not unpleasantly surprised when your bird needs medical attention.

If you cannot get a referral from a friend or your present vet, try asking the breeder from whom you are purchasing your bird. Also, many bird shops give out free literature on bird care and you may find a list of avian veterinarians there. Again, make an appointment and get to know any vet recommended to you.

The well-bird checkup after the purchase of your bird should be done

First Aid Kit.

as soon as you can get an appointment. Check your seller's guarantee for any time requirements and make sure you arrange the visit within it. If you don't, you may invalidate any guarantee your seller gives, or you may have a sick bird and not know it, or both.

The initial exam should consist of a thorough check of the entire bird by the vet. You and the vet will decide what tests to run, if any, and what inoculations to administer. Some vets prefer to do blood work and x-rays on this first visit, in order to have a baseline on the bird for the future. You and the doctor must discuss what will be done according to what he/she prefers and your pocketbook. Medical care is not cheap, but your baby bird, if kept healthy, should live many years, and the cost of medical care spread over two or three decades is a small price to pay for this longevity.

Providing all goes well at the initial checkup, your bird should not need a veterinarian for a year. Of course, birds sometimes get sick, but with the proper care and diet, and barring accidents, the annual physical should be the next time you see the doctor. And there should be a physical every year thereafter.

Birds are absolute geniuses at hiding illness. The reason is that they are prey animals in the wild and to show any sign of illness or weakness makes them a first target for predators. So they will do everything in their power to hide the fact that they are ill or even just not feeling up to par. That's why a bird is only sick when you are not looking. A sick bird will be lethargic and sit with feathers puffed up for warmth. However, when you walk into the room the bird will act as normal as possible in order to disguise sickness. This can create a problem because you may not know a bird is ill until it cannot hide it anymore and then it can be too late.

You must get to know your bird well. How it greets you in the morning, how it plays with its toys, how it interacts with you and your family and any other birds in the house, how quickly or slowly it dives into its food dish when fed, how often and what part of the day it naps are all part of what you must keenly observe at all times. Any deviation from the norm is cause to take a closer look. Because birds are so good at hiding illness, my belief is that it's better to be safe than sorry. This could be called paranoia, but to me it's insurance. I'd rather bother the vet and spend some money and find out my bird is fine and just having an off moment or off day, than wait and find out it is really ill, possibly critically.

So be alert. At the first sign of something amiss, take a closer look and decide for yourself what you should do. There are many signs of illness. A bird who sits quietly, all puffed up when it's normally active; a bird who stops eating; who holds a foot or wing in a strange position (sign of injury); who sleeps excessively, or whose droppings are not as they usually are; a bird who vomits, or bleeds from any part of the body. These are all signals that you need to see a vet quickly.

Some of the above signs are indications of an emergency situation. Other emergencies can occur. Any bleeding what-

soever, from anywhere on the body, must be stopped quickly, or emergency medical care is required. Others consist of broken limbs, flying into any object like a door or wall or mirror, getting burned by falling into a hot pot on the stove or touching the hot burners, getting trapped in the washer or dryer, being bitten by a cat or dog, blood in the droppings, extreme lethargy, sitting on the bottom of the cage, falling into the toilet, chewing electrical cords, chewing anything toxic (including house plants and painted surfaces), bites suffered in fights with other birds. The list goes on and on. Included is any exposure to lead or zinc. Accidents can happen at any time, and are more likely to occur with Caiques because they are so active. Your bird can become tangled in shredded rope, or can get its toe caught in the links of a chain.

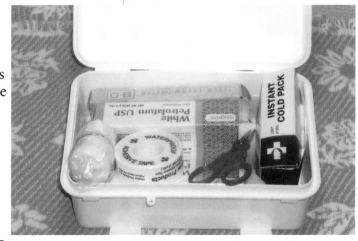

Inside of First Aid Kit.

Exposure to overheated Teflon can be very quickly fatal to your bird. This danger is present in pots and pans, irons, waffle irons, hair dryers, and self-cleaning ovens. Any nonstick surface is lethal.

Overhead fans constitute a danger, along with pesticides, hair spray, cleaning supplies, oil-based paints and varnishes, cigarette smoke, and burning candles, among many other household items.

Keep a bird first-aid kit handy in your home and take it with you if you travel with your birds. It should include blunt-nosed scissors, nail clippers, Kwikstop for bleeding nails, cornstarch for bleeding anywhere else on the body, tweezers, bottled water, vet wrap, alcohol swabs, a hemostat and syringes. Learn how to treat small wounds and broken blood feathers yourself. First, you should attempt to stop the bleeding of a broken blood feather at the tip where it broke off. Wrap your bird gently in a towel and put cornstarch in the open end of the shaft that's bleeding. If this works, fine. If not, you need to pull the feather at the skin. It sounds horrible, but is not that difficult. It hurts the bird, but only for a second. It's similar to pulling out a single strand of your own hair.

The way to pull the feather at the skin is to again wrap your bird gently in a towel. It's helpful to have another person assist you in this; one of you holds the bird in the towel, the other pulls the feather. First, wet the area where the feather grows. This will allow you to separate the feathers from each other so you can pull the correct one. Follow the bleeder up to the skin. Take the hemostat and put it around the feather as close to the skin as you can get, and squeeze the feather. Then pull hard straight down as the feather grows. The whole shaft will come out of the skin. If bleeding continues from the skin, put a little cornstarch on it to stem the bleeding; make sure it has stopped before releasing your bird. If you don't have a hemostat, needle-nosed pliers will work. Make sure you sterilize either with a little alcohol before using. If the skin continues to bleed after you've attempted to stop it, take the bird to your vet immediately. This rarely happens. Usually, the bleeding stops rapidly once the feather is out.

CHAPTER 9
Joys of Caiques:
Treatment for depression or a short trip to the loony bin

One of the most enjoyable aspects of owning Caiques is watching them play. There is never a dull moment with these birds, and you can spend hours just watching their antics. Of course, the more birds in one group, the more activity, and the more fun for you. But even one bird can provide hours of laughs. These birds have no "off" switch, and there will be moments when you'll wish they did. A favorite expression around my house is, "Would somebody pull the batteries on those birds!" (but only when they get so overloaded with excitement that they are making a racket). Most of the time, you will love watching them play, swing, fight with their toys, and hop all over their cages.

Playing with the birds is also a great joy. They love to be with you, and to use your whole body as a jungle gym. They will hang off your clothes, make holes in everything you wear, chew your jewelry, and best of all, spend hours surfing in your hair. You will be hard-pressed to get a comb through your hair after a surfing session.

Caiques are not known as cuddly birds, but the fact is, they do love to cuddle, just not for very long periods at a time. Just before bedtime is a good time for a quick cuddle. Sometimes, they will also settle down for a little neck nuzzling while you watch television. But you must remember, they do not stay quiet or cuddly for long. After a few minutes, there is always something that captures their attention, and off they go into another round of fun and excitement. It has been said that these birds have constant energy, and it's basically true until they settle down in darkness for the night.

Gracie inspecting a coffee cup.

Satchmo and Phoebe kissing.

A word of caution about violent play is in order. This has been mentioned earlier in this book, but is worth pointing out again. If you are introducing two Caiques to each other, with the idea of housing them together eventually, you must use caution. But it is difficult to decide when to interfere when the birds get into a squabble, and when not to. They must establish a dominance hierarchy, and there can be lots of screaming and yelling during this process. You need to keep a close eye on them at first to make sure no one is getting hurt, and be ready to separate them immediately if they are.

The best method for introducing the birds is to put their separate cages next to each other. When you see them show interest in each other, let one bird out on top of its cage while the other is securely locked in. Keep a close eye here too, to make sure the caged bird does not bite the feet of the wandering bird. If all is peaceful, confine the first bird in its cage and let the other out on top to wander around. Again, you must keep a close eye on the interaction. If there is any problem, separate the birds immediately.

In most cases, this process goes smoothly, and you can repeat it every day for a while. When you feel confident that the birds are comfortable in each other's presence, you can let them both out at the same time. Again, watch carefully. You should be able to tell if they are establishing

Satchmo and Phoebe—Best Friends.

dominance or fighting. In the struggle to be top bird, one will give up and walk away after a few seconds and peace will be restored. This may repeat itself many times before both birds are happy with the situation. Then you can put them in the same cage together, preferably a neutral one, and watch carefully. It is best not to let them sleep in the same cage until you feel very sure that they are getting along well.

This leads me back to violent play. Caiques play so roughly together that it can sound like the end of the world has arrived. It is my belief that these birds NEED to play like this and that it's a natural behavior for them. Therefore, the last thing you should do is separate them when you hear the noise. As long as you are confident that they will not hurt each other, let them scream and yell and play like they were killing each other. They will soon tire of the game and go on to something else. Caiques have the attention span of a flea when playing games, which is not to say they can't be tenacious about some things. They will be highly indignant if you take something away from them that

they want, or refuse to give them something they want. And they will persist in trying to get their own way until you give up in exhaustion, or remove the object from their view to make them forget about it.

A great example of their ability to remember things you don't want them to remember is the story of my "Deeny" and a grooming episode. My husband and I groomed her by trimming her flight feathers and clipping her nails. We accidentally clipped one nail a little short and drew blood. I know this hurts for a second when it happens, but Deeny never forgave us for this assault. For a good two weeks after, she would instantly raise her foot in the air when we walked into the room, indicating that she was in pain. The funniest part of all this was, one day when I walked in she lifted the wrong foot! What a little drama queen! But you can see the personali-

Lucy, Phoebe, and Hoover "taming" the carrot.

ty of the species in this story. And you cannot help but love them for these endearing qualities.

The final word on Caiques is that they are an absolute joy to be owned by. You don't ever own a Caique, it owns you. And you will never be sorry, whether you have one, two, or more. They are not considered good for first-time bird owners, but this is controversial. They are definitely not good birds for children, because owning a Caique is almost a guarantee of an occasional bite. These birds need understanding and patience, and lots of love, and common sense. They do not know they are small birds, and need firm guidance to learn what is acceptable and what isn't.

Here I want to quote Sally Blanchard, well-known behaviorist, writer of several books, editor of the Companion Parrot Quarterly, and owner of companion parrots, including a Caique, for many years. She says: "It is the conflict between natural behaviors and an unnatural environment that causes confusion and inappropriate, nonproductive behaviors." This is so true. Birds are not domesticated animals; they are wild. And they do not know how to live in captivity until they are taught. Their wild instincts clash with life in our homes, and we must be aware of what the birds' needs are, and what they are trying to tell us.

So enjoy your Caique. If all goes well you will have a companion for upwards of 30 years.

You will laugh a lot and be healthier for it.

Satchmo and Phoebe
in a serious discussion.

Baby Black-Headed Caiques—
approx. 4 weeks old.

Young White Belly Caique—
approx. 6-7 weeks old.

Vegetables:
Sprouts
Broccoli
Cauliflower
Carrots
Squash
Kale
Spinach
Peppers
Peas
Corn
Beans
Snap Peas
Green Beans
Celery
Lima Beans
Wax Beans

Fruits:
Apples
Oranges
Bananas
Strawberries
Melons
Peaches
Mango
Pears
Kiwi
Papaya
Pineapple
Blueberry
Raisins
Raspberries
Apricot
Coconut
Cranberries
Pomegranate
Dates

Nuts:
Almonds
Cashews
Walnuts
Brazil nuts
Pecans
Pine nuts,

Banana
Papaya
Pineapple
Raisins
Quinoa seed
Apricots
Apples
Peas
Corn
Carrots
Raspberries
Blueberries
Strawberries
Black beans
Cherries
Yogurt drops
Soybeans

Cantaloupe seed
Safflower seed
Buckwheat
Quinoa seed
Milo seed
Oats
Flax seed
Broccoli seed
Garbanzo beans
Amaranth
Lendils
Kamut
Alfalfa leaf

Asbestos
Bleach
Carbon monoxide
Chlorine
Cigarette smoke
Diazanon (DDT)
Flea bombs
Flea collars
Floor polish
Formaldehyde
Hair dye
Hair spray
House paint
Indelible felt-tip marker
Kerosene
Matches
Mothballs
Nail polish
Nail polish remover
Oil paint
Oven cleaner
Overheated nonstick cookware
Paint remover
Perfume
Permanent wave solution
Pesticides
Shoe polish
Spot remover
Spray starch
Suntan lotion
Surgical acrylics
Toilet bowl cleaners
Wax

Abelia	Corn Plant	Lilac
Acacia (some)	Cottonwood	Lily
African Daisy	Crabapple	Magnolia
African Violet	Creeping Jenny	Marigold
Aluminum Plant	Croton	Maidenhair Fern
Aloe-flesh only	Dahlia	Manzanita
Aralia	Dandelion	Monkey Plant
Arbutus	Date	Nandina
Areca	Daylily	Nasturtium
Ash	Dill	Natal plum
Asparagus Fern	Dogwood	Nerve Plant
Aspen	Donkey Tail	Norfolk Pine
Aspidistra	Dracaena	Parsley
Baby's Tears	Dragon Tree	Passionflower
Baby's Breath	Easter Cactus	Peppermint
Bachelor Buttons	Elderberry-cooked fruit	Peperomia
Barberry	Elm	Petunia
Beech	European Fan	Prayer Plant
Begonia	Fir	Purple Passion
Birch	Gold Dust Dracaena	Pyracantha
Bird's Nest Fern	Echeveria	Rose
Blood Leaf Plant	Elephant Foot Tree	Rubber Plant
Boston Fern	Eucalyptus	Russian Olive
Bougainvillea	Eugenia	Schefflera
Bromeliads	Gardenia	Sensitive Plant
California Holly	Gloxinia	Spearmint
Calamint	Grape Ivy	Spider Plant
Calendula	Hens and Chicks	Spruce
Camellia	Hibiscus	Star Jasmine
Chamomile	Honeysuckle	Swedish Ivy
Chickweed	Hoya	Thistle
Chicory	Impatiens	Violet
Claw Cactus	Indian Hawthorne	Wandering Jew
Coffee Tree (not coffee!)	Jade	Willow
Coleus	Larch	Yucca
Comfrey	Lemon Balm	Zebra Plant

Acokanthera
Amaryllis
Angel's Trumpet
Apricot-pits, leaves, bark
Apple-seeds, leaves, bark
Avocado
Azalea
Balsam Pear
Baneberry
Bittersweet
Belladonna
Black Locust
Boxwood
Buckthorn
Burdock
Buttercup
Caladium
Calla Lily
Catclaw Acacia
Caster Bean
Cherry-pits, leaves, bark
Chinaberry
Clematis
Coral Plant
Crocus
Daffodil
Daphne
Death Camas
Delphinium
Devil's Ivy
Dieffenbachia
Eggplant-unripe/overripe fruit, leaves
Elderberry-roots, leaves, stems, bark
Elephants Ears
Figs
Four O'clock

Foxglove
Heliotrope
Henbane
Holly-leaves, berries
Horse Chestnut
Horse Nettle
Hyacinth
Hydrangea
Iris
Ivy-Boston, English
Jack-in-the-Pulpit
Jerusalem Cherry
Jessamine Yellow
Jimsonweed-leaves, seeds
Jonquil
Juniper
Kalanchoe
Lantana
Larkspur
Laurel
Lily of the Valley
Lobelia
Locoweed
Lupine
Marijuana
Milkweed
Mistletoe
Moonseed
Monkshood
Morning glory-seeds
Mushrooms
Narcissus
Oak
Oleander
Peach-leaves, seeds, bark
Pear-leaves, seeds, bark

Peony
Periwinkle
Peyote
Philodendron
Pigweed
Plum-leaves, pit, bark
Poison Hemlock
Poison Ivy
Poison Oak
Poison Sumac
Poinsettia
Poppy
Pokeweed
Potato-sprouts, leaves, berries, green tubers
Pothos
Primrose
Ragwort
Red Maple
Rhododendron

Rhubarb-leaves
Rosary Pea
Sage
Shamrock Plant
Skunk Cabbage
Snowdrop
Sorrel
Spurges
Star of Bethlehem
Sweet Pea
Tobacco
Tomato-stems, leaves
Tulip
Virginia Creeper
Vetches
Water Hemlock
Waxberry
Wisteria
Yew

1. Blanchard, Sally. *The Beak Book.*
      Alameda, CA: PBIC, Inc., 2002

2. Blanchard, Sally. *Companion Parrot Handbook.*
      Alameda, CA: PBIC, Inc., 1999

3. *Bird Talk Magazine*
      P.O. Box 6050, Mission Viejo, CA 92690

4. *Companion Parrot Quarterly*
      PBIC, Inc., P.O. Box 2428, Alameda, CA 94501

5. Athan, Mattie Sue. *Guide to a Well-Behaved Parrot.*
      Hauppage, NY: Barron's Educational Series, Inc., 1999

Recommended Resources

Avian Publications
6380 Monroe Street, NE
Minneapolis, MN 55432
USA

www.avianpublications.com

944447